Audubon
BIRDS OF AMERICA

Audubon
BIRDS OF AMER

INTRODUCTION AND COMMENTARIES BY
ROGER TORY PETERSON

AN **Artabras** BOOK

CROWN PUBLISHERS, INC. NEW YORK, N.Y.

On the Jacket:

MALLARD

Commentary on page 30

On the Title Page:

FLAMINGO

Commentary on page 40

Library of Congress Cataloging in Publication Data

Peterson, Roger Tory, 1908-
Favorite Audubon birds of America.

   1. Birds—United States—Pictorial works.
I. Title.
QL682.P47   598.2'97   78-17307

ISBN 0-517-53545-9

Permission for the reproduction of fifty of these prints has been granted by the Art and Architecture Division, The New York Public Library, Astor, Lenox and Tilden Foundations; the remaining reproductions are through the courtesy of the Audubon Society.

Printed and bound in U.S.A.

CONTENTS

AN APPRECIATION OF AUDUBON

by ROGER TORY PETERSON

T HE NAME OF AUDUBON has long been synonymous with birds, but in recent years it has come to have a broader connotation. This is because the great national organization that bears his name has gone through a philosophical metamorphosis. Birds and bird-watching became the precursors of environmental awareness and therefore Audubon has become a symbol of the conservation movement.

John James Audubon, in a sense, was the father of American ornithology although Alexander Wilson, the Scot, is usually accorded that distinction, having published his own encyclopedic work on American birds about twenty years earlier. Actually, Mark Catesby preceded them both by many years. His *Natural History of Carolina, Florida, and the Bahama Islands,* published in 1731, depicted 113 birds and established him as the first real ornithologist of America.

But the thing that separated Audubon as an artist from his predecessors was that he was the first to take birds out of the glass case and give them the simulation of life. The others portrayed them stiffly as though they were on museum pedestals. To give his birds vitality and movement, Audubon worked from freshly killed specimens, wiring them into lifelike positions. In his youth he had tried hundreds of outline sketches but found it difficult to finish them. He fashioned a wooden model, "a tolerable-looking Dodo. . . . I gave it a kick, broke it to atoms, walked off, and thought again."

It was then that he conceived the procedure he was to follow for many years. He wrote:

"One morning I leapt out of bed. . . . went to the river, took a bath and returning to town inquired for wire of different sizes, bought some and was soon again at Mill Grove. I shot the first kingfisher I met, pierced the body with wire, fixed it to the board, another wire held the head, smaller ones fixed the feet. . . .

there stood before me the real kingfisher. I outlined the bird, colored it. This was my first drawing actually from nature."

The saga of Audubon has been told many times, with variations. It is not exactly a Horatio Alger tale of rags to riches, because the fledgling Audubon was given a young gentleman's tutoring and was all but spoiled by an indulgent stepmother.

Jean Jacques Fougere Audubon was born in 1785 on the island of Santo Domingo in the West Indies. He was the son of a prosperous French sea captain and a young French-Creole lady, Mademoiselle Rabin, who died before the captain returned to his home and wife in France. How he explained his transgression to Madame Audubon is not known, but she took the four year old boy to her heart as her own.

It may have been to escape conscription in Napoleon's army or perhaps to avoid the stigma of illegitimacy that Captain Audubon sent his son at the age of eighteen to Mill Grove near Philadelphia where he owned property.

In France the youngster had studied drawing for six months under the guiding hand of the famed Jacques Louis David and this skill could not be suppressed. The birds of America fascinated him and drawing them became an obsession from which he never freed himself.

After marrying Lucy Bakewell at Mill Grove he moved westward to Louisville, Kentucky, where his father had set him up in business. But business was not in his blood, or so it seemed. It must be admitted that times were uncertain and investment risky on the frontier in those days. Moving further westward to the Mississippi and then down to New Orleans he met successive reverses until he was almost reduced to penury.

In reviewing this difficult period he wrote that "birds were birds then as now. . . . I drew, I looked on nature only; my days were happy beyond human conception." He had conceived a grandiose plan of painting all of the birds of North America—at least all of those then known—and at no time did he lose sight of this goal. After he was away from his family for months exploring the wilderness, painting and pursuing his dream, his devoted Lucy, who had borne him two sons, kept home and hearth together by teaching. He himself eked out a living as an itinerant portrait painter and by giving dancing and fencing lessons.

As his portfolio bulged he began to look for a patron or publisher, but he could find none in New York or Philadelphia. No one would risk the capital. He decided that there might be a better chance of success in England, so with Lucy's savings as a teacher and some money he had managed to acquire by painting portraits, he set sail in 1826.

Abroad he was acclaimed immediately. The rough, colorful man from the American frontier was a sensation. He fascinated the genteel patrons of the art salons in London, Edinburgh and Paris. Long ahead of his time in the art of showmanship and public relations, he played his part well.

William Lizars of Edinburgh agreed to engrave and publish his work but when only ten plates had been finished the colorists went on strike and Audubon was forced to find another engraver. This was Robert Havell, Jr. of London. Audubon was fortunate to be in the hands of such a skilled artist and craftsman. His accomplishment in etching the copper plates was as much a tour-de-force as the original paintings. It is instructive to compare the watercolors that hang in the galleries of the New York Historical Society to the Havell prints with which most of us are familiar.

After three intensely active years in England, Scotland and France, Audubon returned to America in 1829 to paint additional birds, to try for more subscriptions, to travel extensively and to fill in the gaps. Eventually his journeys were to take him from the Gulf Coast and the Florida Keys to Labrador and westward to the foothills of the Rockies.

It took twelve years to bring to completion the publication of the plates and their accompanying text in the *Ornithological Biography.*

It may seem paradoxical that this genius, the epitome of the hunter naturalist, should have become the father figure of the conservation movement in North America. He shot birds like mad, often far more than he needed for his studies. This is well documented in his *Ornithological Biography,* but if one reads on one finds that as Audubon grew older he became disturbed by some of the changes he saw. He pondered the future of certain species and the wild places where they lived. However, this did not restrain him from collecting freely. Shooting practically everything that moved was the thing to do in those days.

Audubon's real contribution was not conservation consciousness, but awareness, which he more than anyone else seems to symbolize. That in it itself is enough; awareness is inevitably followed by concern.

Another paradox is the legend of the unstable and improvident dreamer, the inattentive shopkeeper and itinerant artist who, after the age of forty, made an abrupt turnabout and carried to completion almost single-handedly the most ambitious publishing venture that had ever been attempted by an American.

Madison Avenue would have admired his techniques. To fit the image of the American frontiersman, he wore woodsman's clothing and allowed his hair to grow long over his shoulders. He also became a super-salesman, travelling from city to city to secure subscriptions. Meanwhile, as a sort of production manager he monitored with infinite care the work of the engravers and the corps of colorists.

How could he have been irresponsible and impractical if he could do all this?

A set of Audubon's *Birds of America,* bound in four "double elephant folio" volumes and numbering 435 color plates, could have been purchased by subscription for one thousand dollars when it was published between the years of 1827 and 1838. One hundred years later the same set would have gone on the market for perhaps fifteen thousand dollars. Recently (1977), at auction, the double elephant folio sold for nearly four hundred thousand dollars.

Single prints of some of the more popular subjects such as the wild turkey now sell for several thousand dollars, much more than the original purchase price of the entire collection. On the other hand, certain other prints such as those which depict predators eating their prey go for much less. One of Audubon's most striking compositions (one of my favorites) shows two black vultures feasting on the head of a deer. Because of its macabre subject matter few people would choose such a picture for the living room wall.

Although about 190 sets of the elephant folio editions were issued and distributed, less than half exist today; dealers dismantled the others for sale of individual prints.

It might be pointed out that like many artists of an earlier day Audubon had apprentices. Some of the backgrounds, leaves, flowers and accessories were painted by Joseph Mason, George Lehman and others, but the birds in every instance are the work of the master himself.

The selection presented here are my favorites.

Audubon
BIRDS OF AMERICA

Yellow-Breasted Chat

[ICTERIA VIRENS]

THE versatile chat has been called an acrobat, a clown and a ventrilo-quist. Its strange puzzling calls come from the thickets while the singer remains hidden—clucks, mews, caws, coos and whistles that would do credit to a mockingbird. However, the chat's repertoire is more limited than that of a mocker, with longer pauses between the phrases. The act that caps the climax of the show is the flight song, when, revealing itself at last, the bird ascends with flopping wings and dangling legs, singing wildly, and parachutes back to the briar patch. Audubon, always a careful observer, faithfully records the clowning grotesquerie of the flight song, while he shows below a female brooding amid a bower of sweet-briar roses.

Systematists disagree as to how the chat should be classified. For want of a better solution they have placed it in the warbler family, even though it is 7½ inches long, half again as large as the general run of warblers. However, it acts more like one of the mimic thrushes (the family of birds that include the catbird, brown thrasher, and mockingbird). It likes the same kind of brushy tangles they do, has the same loose-jointed actions, sings and mimics like one, sings on moonlit nights as they often do, and, of course, its flight song suggests that of a mockingbird. Can it be that living as neighbors in the same environment—the same catbriar tangles—produces a similar personality?

Yellow-Breasted Chat

Brown Pelican

[PELECANUS OCCIDENTALIS]

THE serio-comic pelicans with their accordion-pleated pouches are the delight of every tourist who visits the beaches of Florida or California. The most popular pelicans of all are perhaps those who make the municipal pier at St. Petersburg their headquarters, patiently sitting on their posts until someone offers a handout. At once profoundly dignified, as birds of such ancient lineage should be, they are at the same time masters of deadpan clowning, particularly when two or three birds contend for the same fish. This little group of brown pelicans who prefer begging to an honest living probably nest with the hundreds of their kind who resort to the mangrove islands out in Tampa Bay. There are eight or ten such rookeries in Florida, and several others in the Carolinas and along the Gulf. On the Pacific side they do not breed north of California.

Pelicans fly in orderly lines, close to the water, flapping, then sailing, each bird taking its cue from the bird in front of it, as if they were playing follow-my-leader. Fishing, the big birds fly aloft, spot the schools of small fry, and facing downwind, pull their wings back and plunge beak-first with a grand splash. The brown pelican, which is the state bird of Louisiana, has a wingspread of six and a half feet. It is strictly coastal, whereas the white pelican, which has a wingspread of nine, nests far inland in the western half of the continent.

Brown Pelican

Cedar Waxwing

[BOMBYCILLA CEDRORUM]

HOW differently were song birds regarded in Audubon's day! The gentle waxwings were sought for the table by every epicure, and the great ornithologist tells of a basketful of these little birds that were forwarded to New Orleans as a Christmas present. They never reached their destination because the steward of the steamer on which they were shipped made pies of them for his passengers.

An inch or so longer than a Sparrow, the cedar waxwing is the sleekest, "most tailored" of all our birds, a mixture of soft browns and grays, with a pointed top-knot and a yellow band on the tip of its tail. Little red scales, like sealing wax, adorn the tips of some of the wing feathers and give the bird its name. It might be called a "songless songbird," for the only sounds to escape its ungifted syrinx are thin lisps.

Few birds are more nomadic; one year if the berry crop is good, many will winter in New England, Utah or the State of Washington; the next year some might travel as far as Central America or Panama. They return to the northern states and Canada late, and as befits their casual procrastinating nature, wait until summer is half spent before settling down to the essential task of perpetuating their kind. Feeding their young, they always remind me of pinball machines, producing berry after berry from their distended crops, until a dozen or more have appeared as if by magic in their bills.

Cedar Waxwing

Gray Kingbird

[TYRANNUS DOMINICENSIS]

THE best place to see the "gray tyrant," as Audubon called it, is in the Florida Keys. There during the summer months it is abundant, sitting on the wires that follow the Overseas Highway. I saw my first one at the airport in Miami, perched atop the tailfin of a Pan American Clipper that had just flown in from Cuba. Somehow this seemed symbolic, for a month earlier, in April, the kingbird had made this same oceanic flight from its winter resort in the West Indies.

Although in Florida the Keys suit them best because they are like the islands in the Caribbean where the species is most at home, gray kingbirds can be seen along both coasts of the peninsula—a few even in the northern parts of the state. They look much like the ordinary kingbirds so familiar along roadsides everywhere in the east, but have a big-billed, bull-headed look and are of a pale washed-out gray color, without the band of white on the tip of the tail, that marks the eastern kingbird. They are just as hot tempered as their slaty-backed northern brethren, sallying forth to meet wandering crows or hawks, strafing, dive-bombing, and swearing at them in kingbird fashion. Their cry, not so strident as that of the eastern kingbird, has given them the nickname "pipiry flycatcher." All kingbirds belong to the flycatcher family, and sit on exposed perches as flycatchers do, waiting until insects fly by.

Gray Kingbird

Roseate Spoonbill

[A J A I A   A J A J A]

SHELL pink with deep carmine "drip" along its shoulders, the roseate spoonbill is one of the most breath-taking of the world's weird birds. Living in the mangrove swamps it wades the marl flats, rhythmically swinging its flat bill from side to side and sifts out the killifishes, prawns and other small water creatures.

In Audubon's day spoonbills were numerous in the Gulf states from Florida to Texas, and although their rosy wings were sold commercially for fans in St. Augustine, they did not interest plumage hunters as much as the egrets whose filmy nuptial sprays were in such demand. But they were big pink birds that lived with the egrets and so were tempting targets. In the years that followed, particularly in the years after the Civil War, they rapidly disappeared, and before the end of the century not one still bred in Texas and perhaps not two dozen in Florida. If it were not for the fact that some spoonbills still lived south of the border the species surely would have followed the passenger pigeon and the Carolina paroquet into the black void of extinction. During the 1920's little flocks wandered across the Mexican border into Texas, and when they tried to nest the National Audubon Society extended a helping hand by sending wardens to watch over them. By 1941 there were 5,000 spoonbills in Texas. The Florida birds have also done better during recent years, especially in the Florida Keys and in the Everglades National Park.

Roseate Spoonbill

Black-billed Magpie

[PICA PICA]

THE explorers Lewis and Clarke, on their historical expedition, were the first to record the magpie in the United States. They saw their first ones near the great bend of the Missouri, and more as they proceeded westward. Although magpies are found over a large part of Europe and Asia, in our country they are confined to the mountains and valleys of the West, particularly the arid sage-brush country. There, around the ranches, they are a striking sight as they fly with level flight across the fields, white wing patches flashing and long tails streaming out behind. From beak to tail they measure about twenty inches.

At this stage of Audubon's work the West was still in the period of exploration. Many new birds were yet to be described, and because he could not set foot on all parts of the continent, he abandoned his earlier resolve to paint only from fresh specimens that he himself had taken. The black-billed magpie falls in this group. Some western birds were received from friends who were not always sure of the bird's origin. Thus Collie's magpie-jay, a magnificent long-tailed bird of southern Mexico, was mistakenly recorded by Audubon as coming from the Columbia River, and Morton's finch, a Chilean bird, from California.

Modern ornithologists may criticize Audubon for these inaccuracies, but the fact remains that he was perhaps the greatest American ornithologist of his or any other period, a trail breaker when our country was still a wilderness.

Black-billed Magpie

Great Blue Heron

[ARDEA HERODIAS]

ONE of the most ambitious publishing ventures of all time, Audubon's *Birds of America* appeared in four huge volumes, the heaviest of which weighs fifty-six pounds. The page size, 26½ by 39½ inches before trimming, was termed "elephant folio," and as it was Audubon's desire to show every bird, swan or hummingbird, life size, his ingenuity was sometimes taxed to the limit. In this portrait of a great blue heron, he has solved the problem of fitting the gangling bird onto the page by dropping its head in a graceful sweep to its feet.

Four feet tall, the statuesque great blue heron stands motionless in the shallows, waiting until a fingerling or a frog ventures close enough to spear with a lightning thrust. From coast to coast, and from the Gulf of St. Lawrence to the Gulf of Mexico, this gaunt wader is familiar to people who live near the water. Many call it a "crane," but cranes are more restricted to the inland prairies and always fly with their necks stretched full length. The great blue heron in flight pulls its neck into a comfortable loop, tucking its head back to its shoulders. Both birds have a wing-spread equal to that of an eagle.

High in the tall trees of swampy woodlands herons build their rickety platforms of sticks. Hundreds often gather from miles around to form a single heronry, for like many other water birds they find security in numbers.

Great Blue Heron

Mourning Dove

[ZENAIDA MACROURA]

IN flowery words, describing this flowery scene, Audubon wrote: "On the branch above, a love scene is just commencing. The female, still coy and undetermined, seems doubtful of the truth of her lover, and virgin-like resolves to put his sincerity to the test, by delaying the gratification of his wishes. She has reached the extremity of the branch, her wings and tail already opening, and she will fly off to some more sequestered spot, where, if her lover should follow with the same assiduous devotion, they will doubtless become as blessed as the pair beneath them."

Nature writers of an earlier generation almost always wrote in this vein, seeing human thoughts and emotions mirrored in wild creatures. Birds became little people dressed in feathers. Although "humanizing" the animals made them more appealing, it distorted the truth and retarded our understanding of wildlife. True, some of the same natural laws control both birds and men, but modern behaviorists find that birds have a psychology of their own, quite unlike ours.

The mourning dove, or Carolina turtle dove, as it was called in Audubon's day, is found in every state in the Union, and were you to drive across the country in summer you would probably see it beside the road on more days during your journey than any other bird. Smaller and slimmer than a domestic dove, its pointed tail is its best mark. Its call, a mournful *ooah, cooo, cooo, coo,* fades in the distance to three ghostly *coos.*

Mourning Dove

Anna's Hummingbird

[CALYPTE ANNA]

WHO was Anna? Was she a little girl who lived long ago, perhaps the small daughter of the naturalist who first described this species? Or his wife? Actually the facts have a much more intriguing flavor. Lesson, a Frenchman of Audubon's era, who wrote a monograph on the hummingbirds, noticed a new jewel among the shipment of hummers that he had just received from Mexico. With a romantic flourish he honored a lady of his acquaintance, Anna, the Duchess of Rivoli, by bestowing upon it her name. So to this day, Californians who watch the little creature buzzing about the hibiscus in their gardens and who know it by name, pay lip service to the memory of an unknown lady in a distant land.

Whereas eastern North America possesses only one hummingbird, the ruby-throat, California boasts six. Anna's hummingbird is the largest of the lot (about four inches long) and is the only one with a red forehead. When winter approaches, the other Californian hummers withdraw into Mexico, toward the land of their origin where they consort with the more tropical members of their family, but Anna's, relieved of competition, darts about the California gardens all winter long, visiting even the smallest gardens in the heart of town. Males have a "song," if their high squeaky notes can be called that, and also an aerial display during which they zoom back and forth as though swinging on the end of an invisible pendulum.

Anna's Hummingbird

Mallard

[ANAS PLATYRHYNCHOS]

THE green-headed "puddle ducks" in the parks are mallards; so are the white "Pekin ducks" on the farm; in fact nearly all domestic ducks are descended from the wild mallard—the most widely distributed, perhaps the most numerous, and certainly the most hunted duck on earth. On our continent it is common wherever there are lakes and marshes except in the extreme northeast, from New England north. There the black duck (a brother under the skin) replaces it.

There is no doubt that there were once more mallards. In 1832 Audubon found them in Florida in flocks that darkened the air. There are still great flocks today, and I myself have seen a gathering of two-thirds of a million on a refuge in Illinois. But a continental population of all ducks that may have numbered between 200,000,000 and 500,000,000 in Audubon's day (just a guess) dropped to 55–60 million in 1978. The reason is obvious. From a few hundred thousand guns at most in Audubon's era the duck hunting pressure has increased to millions. The ducks could not keep pace; on the contrary—during those years 100,000,000 acres of marshland, the duck nurseries of the continent, were drained for agriculture to help feed the explosively increasing human population. Like rising taxes, it is no accident that the daily bag limit of ducks has dropped from twenty-five per man some many years back, to a mere *four* in the past 30 years. There just aren't enough ducks to go around.

Mallard

Roseate Tern

[STERNA DOUGALLII]

NO bird of land or sea is more buoyant, more skillful in the air, than this exquisite tern. Gulls are clumsy by comparison. When Audubon saw his first roseate terns at Indian Key in Florida, he remarked: "I thought them the hummingbirds of the sea, so light and graceful were their movements." Other writers since have made a more apt comparison, nicknaming them "sea swallows."

Terns are among the most cosmopolitan birds in the world. They wander the seven seas at will, snatching tiny fish from the surface or diving for them like kingfishers. The different kinds look much alike, with jet black caps and forked tails, but this distinguished member of the clan is more streamlined than the rest, with a longer tail and, in May, a soft peach-colored "bloom" on its breast.

The distribution of the roseate tern is strangely spotty. Found here and there along the Atlantic coast, the main group nests on certain little islands off southern New England and about Long Island Sound. South of there it is almost unknown until the Florida Keys are reached. It also lives in Bermuda, Venezuela, on islands off the coasts of Europe and Africa, in India, Ceylon and China. Hundreds of miles separate some of the colonies, to which the birds are drawn as if by a magnet. Why they should resort to certain ancestral bars and islands while unaccountably avoiding thousands of others that would seem equally suitable, is a mystifying habit.

Roseate Tern

Key West Quail-Dove

[GEOTRYGON CHRYSIA]

WHEN Audubon visited the Florida Keys in 1832 several West Indian doves made regular visits to these tropical isles. On May 6th, with a Sergeant Sykes who was stationed at Key West, he secured a dove new to him, the bright rusty bird which he has portrayed here among lavender morning glories. These richly-colored doves hid in the dense thickets of West Indian hardwoods that grew about the shady ponds, and cooed mournfully as all doves do. To his ears their moaning notes sounded like *whoe-whoe-oh-oh-oh*. Later he saw more of them as they crossed the blue-green waters between Cuba and Key West, flying in small loose flocks of five or six to a dozen. By midsummer the doves became numerous enough to enable sportsmen to shoot as many as a score in a day.

Today Key West has been stripped almost bare of its native trees; the town has grown and the Navy has taken over. The Key West quail-dove, ruddy quail-dove, Zenaida dove, and perhaps one or two others that lived in the Keys in those days are gone. Only one West Indian dove, the white-crowned pigeon, still makes its annual pilgrimage across the Gulf from Cuba. It still nests sparingly on some of the small mangrove keys between Key West and Cape Sable. Birds that live on islands are always more vulnerable, more easily exterminated, than birds that reside on large continental areas.

Key West Quail-Dove

Northern Cardinal

[CARDINALIS CARDINALIS]

CARDINALS have been the favorite subjects of bird artists ever since Audubon's day. One modern bird painter tells me that one commission out of every ten he receives is for a portrait of a cardinal. Another confides that he has made at least twenty paintings of cardinals, and that no matter what kind of a job he turns out he can sell it. Bright red birds always have an irresistible appeal, whether they are framed on the living room wall or flying free about the snow-covered food shelf outside the window.

One would think a bird so brightly colored as the cardinal would surely migrate to the tropics, along with the tanagers and orioles, but, on the contrary, a cardinal that spends the summer in a garden is likely to winter there too, probably not wandering more than a quarter of a mile away all year—even in northern Ohio or southern Ontario where the snow lies deep and the temperature drops below the zero mark. But by and large the cardinal is more typical of the southern states, where it vies with the mockingbird for first place in the affections of garden lovers. Perched among the waxy leaves of a magnolia, the male chants in clear slurred whistles—*what cheer, cheer, cheer, cheer, cheer!* Once a favorite cage bird, trapped commercially by tens of thousands, it has grown more numerous and is now a familiar town bird in cities as far north as the Great Lakes and New England.

Northern Cardinal

Great Horned Owl

[BUBO VIRGINIANUS]

THE deep, measured hooting of this nocturnal hunter sounds from the woodlands as dusk settles over the land. Alert to the slightest rustle of a small animal in the shadows, it glides on noiseless wings through the trees, ready to strike quickly.

Its wide yellow eyes and the ear tufts (which have nothing to do with its real ears) give the bird a cat-like look—in fact, in the foggy forests of Newfoundland, lumberjacks call it the 'cat owl'. Distributed widely, it thrives from Labrador and Alaska to South America and varies from near-white at the edge of the Arctic to dusky in more humid regions. It is a resident of every state in the Union and even though it has the handicap of size (nearly two feet long, with a wing-spread of four to five feet), possesses the wits necessary to survive even in settled farming country. I have seen a nest in the rocks on the Palisades close to the George Washington Bridge at the very threshold of New York City. In some places they hide their two white eggs in hollow trees, in others they appropriate old crow's nests. So aggressive is this magnificent predator and so powerful are its spring-trap claws that even an eagle cannot stand up to it. In Florida, one eagle's nest in twenty is commandeered by horned owls each year, and the owners are forced to rebuild their mansions elsewhere.

Great Horned Owl

American Flamingo

[PHOENICOPTERUS RUBER]

IT took Audubon nearly twelve years, from 1826 to 1838, to complete the publication of the original edition of *The Birds of America*. All but the first ten plates were engraved by Robert Havell and his son, of London. When the set was complete there were four huge volumes, the first three containing one hundred plates each, and the fourth, one hundred and thirty-five. These were reproduced by copper plate engraving and colored by hand. Later (1840 to 1844), an octavo edition was published, with sixty-five additional illustrations, bringing the total number to five hundred. But these, lithographed in Philadelphia, were far inferior to the four hundred and thirty-five large copper plate impressions.

Harry Havell, a descendant of the engraver, once showed me some proofs that were used by the colorists. These were not entire prints, but had been cut into irregular pieces, for what reason I cannot say. At any rate, I particularly remember the flamingo on which Audubon had written in pencil, "more red here." Possibly his memory exaggerated this point, for I have always thought he made this bird too deep a color. He had observed many of these grotesque waders in the Florida Keys, but today they are seldom seen away from the Bahamas, unless one goes to Hialeah Park, near Miami, or one of the many parks elsewhere in Florida where wing-clipped birds are kept. These famous captives lost their bright pink when first brought there, but regained it when fed a shrimp diet.

American Flamingo

Passenger Pigeon

[ECTOPISTES MIGRATORIUS]

OVER a century ago the passenger pigeon was probably the most numerous bird in all the world; today it is extinct. Incredible as it seems, it may have outnumbered *all* other birds in the United States combined—hundreds of species. One authority, summing up the evidence, believes that in Audubon's day there were nearly five billion passenger pigeons in the states of Kentucky, Ohio and Indiana alone! From Newfoundland to Florida, early writers told of immense hordes. The great columns in flight, extending for hundreds of miles, blotted out the sun and took as much as three days to pass. Alexander Wilson, sometimes called the father of American ornithology, estimated a flock in Kentucky to contain 2,230,272,000 birds. He considered this far below their actual numbers. He reckoned that if each bird ate a half pint of acorns a day, their daily food consumption would be 17,424,000 bushels! Similarly, Audubon estimated a flock near Louisville at 1,115,136,000 birds.

Accounts of the great roosts read like the tales of a romancer. Trees broke under the weight of the pigeons; thousands of armed men slaughtered day and night and shipped countless barrels to the big cities where they rotted on the sidewalks for want of buyers. The last immense nesting took place in Michigan in 1878. During the next thirty years the remaining flocks dwindled until they were gone. The last passenger pigeon in the world expired at the Cincinnati Zoo at 1:00 p.m. Central Standard Time, September 1, 1914.

Passenger Pigeon

Bald Eagle

[HALIAEETUS LEUCOCEPHALUS]

WHEN Audubon first saw the bird that he glorified in this noble portrait, he believed he had discovered a new species. He wrote: "Not even Herschel, when he discovered the planet which bears his name, could have experienced more rapturous feelings." Audubon named it "The Bird of Washington," and as his reason explained, "I can only say that as the new world gave me birth and liberty, the great man who insured its independence is next to my heart." In reality, the bird he described was not new to science. It was merely an immature bald eagle, a species he should have known well. But this young bird puzzled him; it did not look typical. On the other hand, had it been an adult with its white head and white tail he would have instantly recognized it.

Contrary to legend the bald eagle never snatches up babies, but prefers fish to all other animal food. It likes to be near water, building its huge nests in tall trees near the coast and the Great Lakes, where they often become landmarks. There are more bald eagles in Florida than in any other state, but there are many in the Potomac-Chesapeake area too. Recently an occupied nest was found within the city limits of Washington, D.C., an appropriate site for our national bird. Now protected by federal law and by a growing sentiment, our remaining bald eagles are secure and will not disappear as eagles have done in many European countries.

Bald Eagle

Bachman's Warbler

[VERMIVORA BACHMANII]

NO American bird is more mystifying than this fragile warbler, scarcely more than four inches long. Few living ornithologists have seen it. Discovered by the Reverend John Bachman near Charleston, South Carolina, in 1835, it was described for the world by Audubon. For fifty-three years the little fugitive dropped from sight before it again turned up, this time in Louisiana, but during the succeeding few years, just before the end of the century, hundreds were found. It seemed to be common throughout the river swamps of the south, living in tangled places where trees stood knee-deep in the stagnant pools. Then, before anyone noticed, it again faded away. Very few have been seen during the past forty years.

Even more curious than the history of the bird itself is that of the plant on which it rests, the *Franklinia*. Found on the Altamaha River in Georgia by William Bartram, it would be unknown today if the pioneer botanist had not placed in his saddle bag some slips and seeds which he transplanted to his Philadelphia garden. No one has found the tree in a wild state since 1790, for the almost mythical groves along the Altamaha are gone. The tree, however, might survive longer on this earth than the warbler, for trees can be cultivated, warblers cannot. Although Audubon painted the birds in this composition, Maria Martin (who later became Bachman's second wife) put in the blossoms, drawing them from plants that had come from Philadelphia.

Bachman's Warbler

Fish Crow

[CORVUS OSSIFRAGUS]

ALONE crow on the beach gives pause to the man with a glass. Is it an ordinary crow or is it a fish crow? True, there are three or four inches difference in their sizes, but one can't be sure of size when the bird is standing alone, where there is nothing with which to compare it. But if the bird talks it tells everyone within hearing what kind of a crow it is. If it caws an honest to goodness *caw*, then it is a common crow. If it says *ca* or *cah* in a nasal juvenile sort of way it is a fish crow—the small crow that lives along Atlantic tidewater from Long Island to the Gulf of Mexico. Audubon commented: "At times the sound of their voices seems as if in faint mimicry of that of the common crow, at others, one would suppose that they are troubled with a cough or cold."

Fish crows can be found far up some of the large rivers that drain the Atlantic slope; rivers like the Hudson, Delaware and Potomac which are influenced by the tide. They are numerous around Washington, D. C., where they seem quite at home on the ledges of the Smithsonian, the National Museum and the other government buildings that line Constitution Avenue. No doubt they hunt for pigeons' eggs along these man-made cliffs. In Audubon's day they fearlessly entered every coastal town, but since then they have learned the wary ways of other crows.

Fish Crow

Merlin or Pigeon Hawk

[FALCO COLUMBARIUS]

IN his *Ornithological Biography* Audubon describes a scene on a coastal marsh over which hundreds of gunners are deployed. A pigeon hawk appears, stirring a great flock of blackbirds into flight, and by skillful maneuvering cuts one bird from the flock and captures it. While the panic-stricken blackbirds are milling about, Audubon advises: "Now is your time. Pull your trigger and let fly, for it is impossible, should you be ever so inexpert, not to bring down several birds with a shot." Leaving his comrades to their sport he then returns to the pigeon hawk which he terms "the little marauder . . . bent on foul deeds."

Man in his egocentric fashion has long regarded creatures that compete with him as "marauders." Audubon was no exception. At best, a distinction was made between "good hawks," meaning those that ate mice, and "bad hawks," those that ate birds. But today our thinking about these things is changing. We know that the natural predators have lived in satisfactory adjustment to their prey for thousands of years, and that destroying them will not result in more birds, for then other checks, such as disease or starvation will act as levelers. Only those who are biologically illiterate still shoot hawks as "vermin."

The little pigeon hawk, which I prefer to call the merlin, its original old-world name, is hardly longer than a robin, and lives in the cool Canadian northwoods. It migrates through the United States in open country and along the coast.

Merlin or Pigeon Hawk

Vesper Sparrow

[POOECETES GRAMINEUS]

EACH bird has its own distinctive label. The vesper sparrow's identification tag is its white outer tail feathers which flash conspicuously when it flies. Otherwise it would look rather like a song sparrow or any other little brown bird.

Although Audubon sketched the vesper sparrow, or "bay-winged bunting," as it was called in those days, beside a prickly pear cactus (*opuntia*), it is a bird of the green meadows that stretch across the northern states and southern Canada. Shy, it runs mouselike along the side of the road or pauses behind a weed until its pursuer passes. Then, hopping to the tip of a mullein stalk or a fence post, it sings. Its melody sounds like the brisk lay of a song sparrow but has a minor quality, with two low, clear introductory notes. At dusk, when other voices grow silent, it continues to sing from the fence line until darkness finally stills it.

Our native sparrows are a large family, somber, streaked little birds, but attractive in a modest way. Most of them sing well—some seem almost inspired—and their food habits of small insects and weed seeds make them economically desirable. So do not for a moment put them in the same category with the house sparrow, an immigrant which neither sings nor has too desirable habits. They do not even belong to the same family, for the house sparrow is related to the weaver finches of the old world.

Vesper Sparrow

Whistling Swan

[OLOR COLUMBIANUS]

THE park swan, that floats about in narcissistic adoration, comes from Europe. But we do have two native swans, magnificent untamed birds that were here when the first anchor chains rattled off the coast. One, the trumpeter swan of the northwest, has become one of the rarest North American birds. The other, the whistling swan, is doing very well these days, for it was taken off the list of legitimate game in time to save it. Even though it eats some of the duck food and is a big, tempting target, gunners spare it.

The whistling swan spends the summer north of the Arctic Circle, north and west of Hudson Bay. There might be forty thousand of them or perhaps fifty thousand, scattered in pairs and little groups over hundreds of miles of tundra. When ice begins to lock the bays, long goose-like wedges of them start southward, talking excitedly with whoops and soft trumpeting laughter. Then comes a parting of the ways: one large faction splits off to the west, heading for the great central valleys of California. The rest proceed to the Atlantic, past Lake Huron and Lake Erie, where some rest for awhile, then across the Appalachian ridges to the broad waters of the Chesapeake and the bays of North Carolina. It's a long journey. Occasionally in spring, when returning flocks rest on the Niagara River, birds are carried by the swift current over the falls. One morning two hundred met their death in this way.

Whistling Swan

Blue Jay

[CYANOCITTA CRISTATA]

MANY uncomplimentary things have been said about the blue jay. It has been called a "thief" because it pilfers acorns from the squirrel's cache; a "tease" because it mobs the little blinking screech owl; and a "bully" because it chases other birds from the food shelf. It has even been labeled a "deep-dyed villain" for eating birds' eggs as the trio portrayed by Audubon are doing. But it is a false thing to evaluate wild creatures according to human virtues and failings. For a blue jay to rob a nest is a natural act. Jays have helped themselves to eggs for centuries and still the small birds thrive; their reproductive rate is geared high enough to absorb such losses. If there were no natural checks such as this, there would be so many warblers, vireos and other small birds that their food supply of insects would give out and they would starve—or at least some of them would, until the balance was restored.

There is a "blue jay" of some kind in every state in the Union and in much of wooded Canada, but the three birds pictured here represent the *real* blue jay, a bird larger than a robin, with a blue back, a crest and white spots in its wings and tail. Found from Newfoundland to the Gulf of Mexico, it is replaced in the West by a dark jay with a crest (Steller's jay) and a paler one without (California jay).

Blue Jay

Summer Tanager

[PIRANGA RUBRA]

IN the South there are two "red-birds": the "winter redbird" (the cardinal), which remains all year, and the "summer redbird," shown here. The only two birds in the eastern states that are *all* red, they are easily recognized, for one has a crest, the other has not. From the moss-draped live oaks or the long-leaf pines the summer tanager sings its robin-like phrases, but far more characteristic is the note with which it always announces itself, a staccato *chicky-tuck*, a note unlike that of any other bird. The yellowish female says *chicky-tuck* too, but she does not sing. Occasionally, if a storm sweeps up the coast in April, at the time when summer tanagers are making their hazardous passage across the Gulf, a few are carried as far as New England, but except for such acts of God the summer tanager is an unreconstructed southerner, seldom venturing across the Mason and Dixon Line. The other eastern species, the scarlet tanager, crimson with black wings, is a Yankee by adoption, spending the summer in the oak woods of the northern tier of states and southern Canada.

In Latin America four hundred species of tanagers, garbed in vivid shades of red, blue and yellow, vie with the parrots and trogons in making the tropics gay. Why, out of all this gorgeous galaxy, only two tanagers should be adventurous enough to cross the Gulf of Mexico is one of the many mysteries of migration.

Summer Tanager

Willet

[CATOPTROPHORUS.SEMIPALMATUS]

AT rest on a sandbar or a mud-bank, the willet is a rather non-descript gray or gray-brown shorebird, but when it flies it is instantly transformed by its strikingly banded wings. A flock of willets is a spectacular sight as the birds wheel in unison, displaying their bold black and white wing-patterns.

Audubon thought the willet was strictly coastal, but now we know that the western population is widely distributed on many of the lakes and ponds of the northwestern plains and in the intermontaine valleys of the Rocky Mountain region.

Audubon knew the bird only on the beaches and in the salt marshes along the east coast where its "song," a musical, repetitious *pill-will-willet* was a familiar sound in early summer. There were no laws protecting wading birds at that time, and they were so heavily shot that by the beginning of this century willets no longer were seen from New Jersey to Cape Cod, except for a few that migrated to a disjunct colony in Nova Scotia. Under protection they are slowly repopulating their former range in the Northeast where suitable environment still exists.

Willets lay three or four olive-buff eggs in a grassy cup in the marsh or occasionally above tideline on the beach. They are so loath to leave their spotted treasures unattended that I have been able to touch incubating birds with my hand.

Willet

Painted Bunting

[PASSERINA CIRIS]

LIKE a gaudy tropical flower that has taken wing, the painted bunting livens the gardens on the outskirts of Charleston, Savannah and many other southern towns. Some call it the *nonpareil*, for no other American bird can match its dazzling patchwork of color. It is a bird of the low country, absent from the hills . . . a bird of the thickets and hedgerows, singing its bright pleasing warble throughout the heat of the day as insistently as the indigo bunting does in the thickets further north. The female, lacking the coat of many colors, is just a little green finch, hardly to be noticed by anyone.

The five birds which Audubon has drawn on a sprig of chickasaw plum are engaged in a territorial squabble. In fact, so scrappy are the little brightly colored males, that the Creoles of Louisiana once lured them into trip cages in which they had placed stuffed birds, mounted in belligerent poses. Thousands were caught and sold as cage birds in the markets of New Orleans, and many eventually reached the bazaars of London and Paris. I myself have seen caged painted buntings in the Cuban section of Key West, but it is now illegal to confine them. The great national society which bears Audubon's name has done much to change the attitude of that earlier era towards wildlife. Today sentiment alone is sufficient to safeguard song birds, even though America can boast the best protective laws of any country in the world.

Painted Bunting

Common Bobwhite

[COLINUS VIRGINIANUS]

"VIRGINIAN partridge" was the name Audubon used when he presented this plate in his elephant folio of the *Birds of America*. This, one of his most involved and animated compositions, shows an immature red-shouldered hawk scattering a covey of bobwhite. Today's wildlife management experts would be critical of Audubon for portraying them thus, because no covey of quail would normally expose themselves to predation in such open moorlike terrain. Audubon may be excused for taking artistic liberties in this case because grass and brush, although ecologically correct, would have obscured the dramatic action.

The bobwhite, widespread in the eastern and central states, is undoubtedly the most popular American game bird. Other races or subspecies flourish in Cuba, Mexico and Guatemala. All whistle the familiar *bob-white!* or *poor, bob-white!* In the northern states when these quail have become depleted by exceptionally cold winters game departments have often reinforced their numbers with hatchery-raised stock.

Coveys of quail may wander in loose association throughout the day, but when evening approaches the "covey call" can be heard, a loud whistled *ka-loi-kee!* This is answered by *whoil-kee!* Once assembled they go to bed in a ring with tails together, their heads facing outward. If they are disturbed during the night they explode like a bomb, each bird going in a different direction without bodily interference, avoiding some of the chaos that Audubon has suggested in his painting.

Common Bobwhite

Clapper Rail

[RALLUS LONGIROSTRIS]

FOR hundreds of miles, from Long Island to the Gulf of Mexico, stretch the long beaches, built up of shell and sand, brought from the bottom of the sea by the waves. Behind these barrier islands lie the salt marshes, from one to five miles broad in places. These are the homes of the "salt water marsh hen." There might be hundreds of them in the marsh, but you probably would not see even one if the tide is low, for they are as shy as birds can be, running ratlike through the grass unnoticed. Although they can swim if they have to and can fly if they choose, they would rather use their legs. They are easy to locate, however, when the tide comes in and forces them onto the last high spots, or toward sundown when their clattering *kek-kek-kek-kek-kek* sounds from far and near. Then the marsh seems alive with them, and all night long they answer each other from the sedge.

For many years these palatable fowl, as large as small chickens (fourteen to sixteen inches long), have been favorite gamebirds, hunted up and down the coast. When high storm tides strand them the toll is great, and it is recorded that ten thousand were killed in two days near Atlantic City. Today clapper rails are reduced in number, not alone because of the killing and the egging, but because of a much more potent factor—the drainage of the marshes.

Clapper Rail

Scrub Jay

[APHELOCOMA COERULESCENS]

LOOK only in the drab stretches of scrub oak in Florida for this handsome jay which Audubon has shown among the persimmons. Not so noisy as the blue jay, or rather not so continuously noisy, the scrub jay shows great curiosity when anyone invades the low scrub where it lives, and hopping to a bush top, sits with tail hanging down, watching and talking in low tones to the others of its flock. Alarmed, they all fly off, screaming in rasping accents.

The familiar blue jay lives in Florida too, usually in the bigger oaks where Spanish moss hangs in gray festoons, but it can be distinguished at a glance by its jaunty crest and the white spots in its wings and tail, features which the scrub jay lacks. Long considered a distinct species which has never been recorded outside the peninsula of Florida, the Florida jay is now lumped with the California jay, the crestless jay of the western states, from which it differs only slightly in color. The name "scrub jay" then, is more suitable, one race becoming the Florida scrub jay, the other the California scrub jay.

The *corvidae*, the family to which jays and crows belong, is regarded by many naturalists to be the most intelligent group of birds in the world—birds which will survive against all odds. Persecuted, they have become wary, all except the scrub jay, which is so unafraid that it will take food from the hand of a friend.

Scrub Jay

Yellow-Billed Cuckoo

[COCCYZUS AMERICANUS]

OLD World cuckoos lay their eggs in the nests of other birds. New World cuckoos do not; they have not developed the habit of brood parasitism. The yellow-billed cuckoo, like its congener, the black-billed, builds its own nest, a frail saucer of twigs into which the bird deposits two to four pale blue-green eggs. Although the nest is usually situated in a bush or small tree, I once found one in a clump of royal ferns.

In this spirited composition Audubon has shown the pair in a fruiting pawpaw. One has caught a tiger swallowtail butterfly. The conspicuous "field-marks" are well shown—the rufous in the wing and the large toil-spots that distinguish this species from the similar black-billed cuckoo.

One of Audubon's correspondents noted that cuckoos are much more numerous some years than others, a fact that has been fully confirmed since. It is believed that cyclic outbreaks of tent caterpillars coincide with these fluctuations.

The two similar cuckoos, the yellow-bill and the black-bill, are more often heard than seen. The yellow-bill utters a rapid throaty *ka ka ka ka ka ka ka ka ka ka ka ka kow kowp - kowp - kowp* (retarded toward the end). The black bill has a rythmic *cu cu cu, cucucu, cucucu, cucucu, cucucu*, etc., a melancholy song that can sometimes be heard at night. Country people, believing that their vocalizations signalled rain, once called them "rain crows."

Yellow-Billed Cuckoo

Northern Shoveler

[ANAS CLYPEATA]

THE postures of some of Audubon's birds seem rather contrived, but he may be forgiven because he was always aware of two objectives—to create a dynamic composition and to show as many important details of the bird as he could. Hence the spread wing of the male shoveler which would not have revealed its colorful pattern had the bird been shown at rest or simply walking about.

Shovelers are widespread in the Northern Hemisphere, being found across North America, Europe and Asia, and also (in the winter months) south to northern South America and Africa. In North America the shoveler is much more widespread in the West, breeding from Alaska to California. East of the prairies it is a very local summer resident, but during autumn and winter western birds invade the ponds and marshes of the Atlantic seaboard, mingling with the more abundant mallards, black ducks, pintails, teal and other freshwater dabblers. When swimming, shovelers sit low, their big spoon-shaped bills sifting goodies from the muddy water. In flight the big bill makes the wings seem to be set rather far back as though the bird was not well-balanced. By midsummer the male molts into a drab plumage known as the "eclipse," which is very much like the modest brown plumage of its mate. By the end of summer it commences a second molt in which it regains its bright pattern.

Northern Shoveler

Snowy Egret

[EGRETTA THULA]

THE snowy egret, "the heron with the golden slippers," has become the proudest symbol of the National Audubon Society, the great conservation organization of which John James Audubon is the patron saint. At the beginning of this century the little snowy, loveliest of all American herons, was on the way out. Its exquisite plumes, called "aigrettes" by the trade, were worth $32 an ounce, twice their weight in gold. Every heronry was ferreted out and destroyed. As the birds bore these nuptial sprays only at nesting time, the young birds, bereaved of their parents, perished too, and the stench of death hung heavy over every colony. Where there had been hundreds of thousands of egrets in our southern states there soon remained but a few hundred. The National Audubon Society fought for plumage laws and to meet the emergency hired wardens. The first Audubon warden in South Florida, Guy Bradley, was shot by plume hunters near Cape Sable in 1905. A marker which stands where his body washed ashore reads "Faithful unto death." Under protection the egrets and all the other long-legged waders have made a spectacular comeback. Today snowies by the scores of thousands now nest north to the Great Lakes and southern New England.

Audubon chose for his background a rice plantation in the Carolina "low country." We wonder whether the small figure in the ditch at the right is meant to be Audubon himself, carefully stalking the bird which is to be immortalized as his model.

Snowy Egret

Rufous Hummingbird

[SELASPHORUS RUFUS]

IN the American tropics hummingbirds buzz about the blossoms in bewildering variety. There are 320 species at least, or nearly 700 if one counts the subspecies. Yet of all these, only one, the ruby-throat, crosses the broad waters of the Gulf of Mexico to eastern North America. Although it weighs no more than a copper penny it completes the five hundred mile hop between dawn and dark. Some ruby-throats continue until they reach the Gulf of St. Lawrence and the tiny wanderers have even been seen in gardens in Newfoundland. There is, however, one other member of the family that is an even greater traveler, the rufous hummingbird, portrayed here by Audubon. Swarming northward through the Pacific states in spring, some continue the marathon to Alaska, where they have been recorded as far as the 61st degree of latitude. To equal this the ruby-throat would have to fly to Greenland. In contrast to these two adventurers there are other species so sedentary that they are unknown away from the slopes of a single Andean volcano!

The rufous hummingbird returns to its winter home in Mexico by way of the mountain meadows of the Sierras and the Rockies. There, in summer, the slopes are alive with hummingbirds of three or four kinds. California is visited by six species of hummingbirds and southern Arizona by ten. The rufous hummingbird is the only one of this tribe north of the border that possesses a bright rusty back.

Rufous Hummingbird

Long-Billed Curlew

[N U M E N I U S   A M E R I C A N U S]

IN his earlier paintings Audubon arranged birds and plants so that they made attractive patterns on a white background. There is an oriental print quality in many of his designs even though he was not familiar with the art of the East. Later, midway through his great project, he began to create solid backgrounds, painting in skies, water and landscapes. Perhaps George Lehmann, the Swiss landscape painter who accompanied him on some of his expeditions, helped him with these.

Here, as a setting for two long-billed curlew, Audubon has shown the old city of Charleston, South Carolina. At that time the big "sickle-bill," the largest of all the American sandpipers, was common all up and down the Atlantic Coast and particularly in South Carolina. Audubon wrote that it nested there, but naturalists today believe he must have been mistaken, as it is by nature a bird of the prairies, coming to the coast when its nesting is through. On the northern Great Plains and on the alkali flats of the Great Basin in Utah and Nevada its wild harsh *cur-lee!* can still be heard on summer days and sizable flocks visit the flats on the coasts of California and Texas. Long absent from the Atlantic Coast it might yet make a comeback, for lately small flocks have again been seen on the Carolina Capes. The ordinary curlew, the whimbrel, does not have the extremely long bill (five to seven inches) that marks this *rara avis*.

Long-billed Curlew

American Robin

[*TURDUS MIGRATORIUS*]

WHEREVER British colonists settled they named certain birds after the familiar birds of town and countryside back home. Hence, in at least half a dozen different parts of the world we find "robins" simply because they have rusty-red breasts, reminiscent of the "robin redbreast" of England.

In pre-Columbian times American robins were primarily forest birds, but early on they took to the towns and shade trees. Undoubtedly the manicured lawns, where earthworms were easier to come by, were partly responsible for this adoption of a new habitat.

But in Audubon's time robins did not enjoy the security that they know today. He writes of the winter sojourn of robins in the South: "Their presence is productive of a sort of jubilee among the gunners, and the havoc made among them with bows and arrows, blowpipes, guns, and traps of different sorts, is wonderful. . . . Every gunner brings them home by the bagful."

It was the destruction of robins as much as anything else that sparked the Audubon movement in the early years of this century. Today it would be unthinkable to shoot a robin; it is perhaps America's most beloved bird, the real symbol of spring to winter-weary northerners. It is free to walk our lawns with no fear except for the neighborhood cats.

American Robin

Common Merganser

[MERGUS MERGANSER]

IN winter scores of mergansers, sometimes hundreds, float on the tidal basin that serves as a reflecting pool for the Washington Monument and the Jefferson Memorial in the City of Washington. The stately white drakes, over two feet long, with glossy green heads and bright carmine bills, accompany the bushy-headed, quaker-gray females. These, the birds that are called goosanders in Europe, and which Audubon called by the old-world name, are the commonest ducks in winter on the rivers of the northern states, especially on those creeks that freeze partly over. There in the open stretches they dive in the swift current, taking care not to come up under the shelf of ice. When they dive they often leap in an arc like a porpoise, and submerging, outswim the small fish by using both their feet and their partly open wings. Unlike most other ducks which have flat mud-straining bills, mergansers have spike-like bills with saw-toothed edges, perfect equipment for holding onto slippery fish.

In this print Audubon has shown a pair of these river-loving ducks in a typical merganser stream at Cohoes Falls in the State of New York. Mergansers spend the summer across the entire width of wooded Canada and make their appearance in the states when cold weather seals the northern ponds with ice. They are fresh-water birds, seldom visiting tidewater except during severe freeze-ups.

The red-breasted merganser is the salt water member of the family.

Common Merganser

Snowy Owl

[NYCTEA SCANDIACA]

THE key to life in the Arctic is the lemming, the little mouse-like mammal that increases so rapidly that even its enemies cannot keep it in check. Periodically when it reaches saturation there is a population crash. The snowy owl waxes fat on the lemming horde in peak years, but when the depression comes it must leave the barren tundra and seek food elsewhere. Flights of these big ghostly owls drift into the United States about one year in four, and at longer intervals invasions of thousands pour across the border.

As one would expect of birds of the midnight sun, they are not as nocturnal as other owls, but fly abroad by day, searching the marshes, the open plains and the dunes along the sea for rabbits and other four-footed fare. So persecuted are they by trophy hunters that few survive the winter to make the return trip. However, one year, four spent the winter successfully at a dump in the Bronx where they caught rats and escaped notice, because at a distance they looked like bundles of newspaper. The fuzzy young of all owls are white and are, therefore, sometimes mistaken for snowy owls.

At home in the far north, the snowy owl has few enemies except the Arctic fox and the Eskimos who find the eggs of *Ookpikjuak* very palatable. There it sits upon its hillock, surveys its bleak domain and intones its baleful booming to the polar sky.

Snowy Owl

American Oystercatcher

[HAEMATOPUS PALLIATUS]

CONTRARY to the impression given by the goggle-eyed bird in this portrait, one does not have to run fast to catch an oyster. The usual technique of the "sea-crow," as the baymen call it, is to stalk about at low tide on the beds of exposed "coon" oysters and disable them with a clip of its big red bill. It is as skillful in opening the reluctant shellfish as any professional oyster-opener.

A foot and a half long, it is one of the largest and most striking of all the shorebirds, flashing great white wing patches when it flies. Little parties, flying from bar to bar, rapidly repeat their piercing whistles— *wheep! wheep! wheep!* Because they attract so much attention to themselves their survival is threatened. Audubon found oystercatchers as far north as Labrador, where he watched them pry limpets from the rocks, and apparently they lived along the entire coast from there to Argentina. Today they are gone entirely from the northeast, and, except for a very few, from Florida as well. To be sure of finding oystercatchers today one must go to Virginia or the Carolinas, or else to the Texas coast. There on the white shelly beaches they still lay their two or three blotched eggs on the naked sand.

Oystercatchers do not migrate much; the birds of the Virginia and North Carolina coasts merely move as far as South Carolina where they augment the big flocks that winter about Cape Romaine.

American Oystercatcher

Gyrfalcon (White Phase)

[FALCO RUSTICOLUS]

IN medieval days when knights and kings rode forth with trained falcons on their wrists, the most valued hawk of all was the gyrfalcon, a prize from the north which could be owned only by those of noblest blood. To say that this bird was worth a king's ransom would not be far from the truth, for it is recorded that Philip the Bold ransomed his son for twelve white gyrfalcons. After the demands had been made by the captors, it took two years, it is said, to round up the twelve birds. Although gyrfalcons are circumpolar, living in the rocky Arctic wastes of Europe, Asia and North America, most white gyrfalcons come from Greenland, where the sea-roving Vikings obtained them as early as the eleventh century. In fact, Greenland was called "the land of the white falcon."

The black, gray and white birds, once supposed to be distinct races, are now regarded as color phases, possible in the same brood of young. The white birds with their Arctic camouflage rarely visit the United States; the others are scarce enough, but now and then one is seen along the New England coast in winter. Two feet long, with a spread of about four feet, they can easily overtake and strike down auks, eiders and other sea birds.

Audubon, who had seen the black gyrfalcon in Labrador, but never a white one, drew the figures in this plate from a bird that had died in captivity.

Gyrfalcon (White Phase)

Canada Warbler

[WILSONIA CANADENSIS]

THE round full script at the bottom of this print in the original elephant folio edition informs us that the two small birds disporting themselves among the rhododendron blossoms are *Canada flycatchers*. There is an evolution in names, even vernacular names, and although some stick, no matter how inappropriate, others change through the years. Many birds portrayed by Audubon are known by different names today than they were then. Usage has dictated some; others have been modified when their relationships became clarified. Thus, in due time, it was decided that the present species was a warbler, not one of the flycatcher family. If the author of every new bird book that came along decided to change some of the names to suit himself, all would be chaos. Hence the scientific organization known as the American Ornithologists' Union, has set up a central authority—the check-list committee—to pass on questions of nomenclature. The names they finally decide on become standard.

The Canada warbler, appropriately named, is common in the damp rocky woods of eastern Canada and along the Appalachian ridges as far south as Georgia. It keeps rather close to the ground in the cool ravines and laurel thickets. Its unmarked blue-gray back and the necklace of short black streaks across its yellow breast make it easy to identify. All warblers have their "field marks" and when the floods of migrants pour northward in spring it is sometimes possible to identify twenty-five species or more in a day.

Canada Warbler

Mangrove Cuckoo

[COCCYZUS MINOR]

WHEN Audubon visited exotic Key West in 1832 he must have been truly inspired, for while there he painted some of his finest pieces— among them the dramatic dove series and this dynamic portrait of a mangrove cuckoo. The old house where he stayed still stands, surrounded by strange tropical trees, perhaps lineal descendants of the very trees whose leaves and blossoms he used in some of his backgrounds.

The mangrove cuckoo, or Maynard's cuckoo as this race is often called, is rather like the familiar yellow-billed cuckoo that lives throughout the southern and eastern states, but its breast is washed with a rich buffy color. About a foot long, much slenderer than a robin, it is a sinuous, long-tailed bird, as all cuckoos are, with slow deliberate movements. A native of Central America and the West Indies, it reaches its northern limits in the Keys and along the southwest coast of Florida. There in this sub-tropical terrain of green keys and turquoise waters, where great white herons wade the shallows and man-o'-war-birds hang motionlessly overhead, it is one of the most characteristic but least known inhabitants. It lives almost unobserved in the wilderness of red and black mangrove, seldom noticed as it slips through the gloomy labyrinth of roots which project like stilts from the salt water. A sharp eye might spot it perching motionlessly on a branch surrounded by masses of leathery leaves.

Mangrove Cuckoo

Fork-tailed Flycatcher

[*MUSCIVORA TYRANNUS*]

ALTHOUGH this streamlined bird lives nowhere near our borders, it has been recorded in our country at least twelve times. Songbirds that live in the West Indies or in northern Mexico might be expected to cross the line once in awhile—birds do not recognize political boundaries—but this is the only bird that lives deep in the tropics that has paid us so many visits. Most of these strays have appeared along the coast or not far from it, suggesting that tropical storms might have carried them northward. Audubon, who was incredibly lucky in the number of rarities he discovered during his lifetime, secured the bird figured here in New Jersey, but the waxy white blossoms of the *Gordonia*, a tree which grows in the southern states, were not added until later.

The normal range of the fork-tailed flycatcher is from southern Mexico to Patagonia, and travelers in the tropics say that it is a very common bird, filling the niche of our kingbird along the roadsides. It has the kingbird's violent temper too, fearlessly chasing every hawk that soars by. Its kingbird-like bickering has the sound of castanets, as one would expect in Latin America. The nearest thing we have to this species in the United States is the scissor-tailed flycatcher of Texas and Oklahoma, a bird equally streamlined, but pale gray in color with a touch of salmon pink on its sides. It has been nicknamed the "Texas bird of paradise."

Fork-tailed Flycatcher

Northern, or Baltimore, Oriole

[ICTERUS GALBULA]

WHEN George Calvert, the first Lord Baltimore, visited the settlement of Virginia he found many birds along the Chesapeake. None, however, had beauty so breath-taking as the flame-colored birds, smaller than robins, which were later to bear his name. Much impressed, so the story goes, he took their colors, orange and black, for his coat of arms.

Although Audubon portrayed them appropriately enough in a tulip tree, Baltimore orioles are particularly partial to elms. However, in some towns the spread of the Dutch elm disease has forced them to use other trees. The nest, deep as a handbag, is hung from the tips of the longest, most sweeping branches, where no cat would venture. One can help the feathered architects by putting out yarn and string, cutting them into lengths not exceeding ten or twelve inches so that the birds won't get tangled in them.

As if following some inviolable schedule orioles make their annual pilgrimage over tropical jungles, across or around the Gulf of Mexico, through the plantations of the Gulf states and ever northward until in early May they reach the elm-shaded towns of the Great Lakes and New England. A few continue into southern Canada. Bad weather might hold them up a little, but not much, and they arrive within a day or two of the same date from year to year. No birds follow the calendar more precisely than those that winter deep in the tropics.

Northern, or Baltimore, Oriole

White-Crowned Sparrow

[ZONOTRICHIA LEUCOPHRYS]

A GLIMPSE of a white-crown is enough to show that it is no ordinary sparrow. Distinguished in mien, with broad black and white stripes on its crown, it lacks the drabness of the common lot. To those of us who live along the Atlantic seaboard, the white-throated sparrow is much more familiar, a bird with similar head stripes, but which has in addition a square white throat patch. We see white-crowns in migration, but not many; a few hop elegantly on the lawns in early May and sing their wheezy lyrical notes from the hedges. These transients are en route to Newfoundland, Labrador and the Hudson Bay country, the very threshold of the Arctic, where the last stunted spruces give way to the tundra.

West of the Appalachians the white-crown is much more numerous during the season of its passage, and in the far West is positively abundant. There it can be heard, even in summer, singing from the edges of every bog in the high mountains. One race breeds on the coast as far south as California. Every garden in the Pacific states is visited by some race of this handsome sparrow.

The plant which Audubon pictured in this attractive design is the summer grape (*Vitis aestivalis*) and the sparrow so furtively peeking from behind the big leaf is an immature individual, one of those tan-looking youngsters with pink bills that show up with their parents in the fall.

White-Crowned Sparrow

Yellow-Bellied Sapsucker

[SPHYRAPICUS VARIUS]

BIRD artists of today, inhibited by their ornithological critics, seldom show the originality so characteristic of Audubon's work. A woodpecker is usually shown clinging to a tree, with its tail braced in traditional woodpecker fashion; it would be considered daring to draw one dangling from a berry-laden branch as Audubon has pictured these sapsuckers. Yet Audubon must have witnessed a scene such as this.

The yellow-bellied sapsucker, an inch or two longer than a downy woodpecker, is the only eastern woodpecker in which the male has a red throat patch. But an easier way to identify it is the longish white patch that extends diagonally down the wing, as shown in the upper bird. This stands out at a distance and is the best field mark. Typical of the Canadian woodlands and the mountain country, the sapsucker is the most migratory of all the woodpeckers, sometimes traveling to the West Indies and Central America.

In a family of highly valuable birds that save millions of dollars of timber annually, this is the only one regarded as harmful; just how harmful we don't know. It has the habit of drilling rows of holes, as evenly spaced up and down "as corn on the cob," and from these pits it gathers the tree's oozing life blood, sapping it up with its brushlike tongue. Downy woodpeckers, squirrels, hummingbirds and butterflies patronize the sapsucker's wildwood bar, and sip the stolen brew when the bartender is away.

Yellow-Bellied Sapsucker

Least Bittern

[IXOBRYCHUS EXILIS]

THIS tiny elusive heron is scarcely the size of a meadowlark but much thinner. Audubon tried an experiment with a live least bittern that a lady brought to him in her apron. He placed two books erect, an inch apart, on a table. The bird easily walked between the two books without moving either of them. Although a least bittern would seem too wide to pass through such a narrow space, it apparently can constrict its body, an ability that enables it to move without hindrance through the dense reeds and cattails.

Were it not for its song, a low, muted cuckoolike *coo-coo-coo*, we might not suspect the presence of this little heron in the marsh. When discovered it may "freeze" or slowly melt into the reeds, relying on its protective coloration to escape notice. When pressed, it reluctantly takes to the air, displaying large buff wing patches. After flying but a short distance, it drops in again to play hide and seek.

Least bitterns share the marshes with the rails which are even more elusive. None of the rails show the conspicuous buff wing patches when they fly. The much larger American bittern is a heavily streaked brown bird which shares the least bittern's habit, when discovered, of standing rigid with its bill pointed skyward, simulating the reeds.

Least Bittern

Rufous-sided Towhee

[PIPILO ERYTHROPHTHALMUS]

MORE than a hundred years ago, in an era when travel was slow and arduous, John James Audubon explored the woods, shores and swamps from Labrador to the Florida Keys and from the Atlantic westward to the upper reaches of the Missouri. During his lifetime he painted about five hundred species of birds, two-thirds of all those ever recorded in North America. Since then the face of the continent has been altered. Some birds have grown rare, several have gone completely, while others like the Towhee, shown here, are probably far more numerous today than they were then. The 'towhee bunting,' as Audubon called it, benefited by the settling of the land. It likes dry brushy places where trees have been cut off and low scrub is reclaiming the naked earth. Birds with such tastes—birds that live in the young growth—have much more elbow room than they had when America was an unbroken wilderness of ancient trees.

The towhee is smaller and slimmer than a robin; black-backed if it is a male, brown-backed if a female. Both have rusty-red sides and show great white spots in their tails when they fly away. There are towhees of one kind or another over most of the United States. The typical eastern bird, shown here, attracts attention to itself by rummaging noisily among the dead leaves, and by its note, a loud *chewink!* Its song sounds to some ears like *drink-your-teeeee.*

Rufous-sided Towhee

White-Winged Crossbill

[LOXIA LEUCOPTERA]

WITH their cross-tipped pruning shears, crossbills snip the rough scales from the spruce cones and deftly extract the flat brown seeds. Strangely erratic in their habits, they are content to stay all winter in the cold forests of Quebec or Alaska if the branches are heavily laden with cones, but in years when the crop is poor they pull out. I have known summers when the woods along the Maine coast were alive with crossbills, calling noisily to each other and flying about in little bands like big goldfinches. The next year I might not see a single one. At intervals—sometimes years apart—flocks wander as far south as the central states, far from their home forests.

Not only are crossbills given to these unpredictable wanderings or "invasions," but they might take it into their heads to nest at any time of the year—even during the bitter days of January when the drifts lie deep over the land and only the long view of things would concede the eventual return of spring. On the other hand their hidden nests in the evergreens have been found during the hottest days of August.

There are two kinds of crossbills in America. The best known is the red crossbill, a dingy brick-red bird, but the handsomest is the white-wing, rosy red or dull pink with broad white wing bars. Audubon has shown two males and two females on an alder twig which he picked in Newfoundland.

White-Winged Crossbill

Wood Stork

[MYCTERIA AMERICANA]

F EW Americans realize that we, in our country, have a native stork, for that is what the wood ibis is. Less trusting than the friendly storks that nest on the roof tops in European hamlets, our wood stork shuns civilization, withdrawing to the deep swamps of the south. The best place of all to see it is far out on the Cape Sable road in the Everglades National Park. This, one of our newest national parks, dedicated to preserving our only large piece of tropical wilderness, does not depend on high mountains, waterfalls or breath-taking vistas for its public appeal as other parks do, but rather on its wildlife, of which the long-legged waders—the glamour birds—are the most conspicuous. Hundreds of egrets and other herons fish in the pools, white ibises trail across the sky in long streamers, but the most striking birds of all are the wood storks. Squadrons pass overhead, stroking the air with their jet-black wing tips; hundreds more wade the shallows, driving before them the myriads of small fish with which the glades abound. Frogs, water snakes and baby alligators alike are gobbled up by the advancing phalanx.

The nesting colonies, in Florida, are difficult to reach without a guide. A nursery such as the Corkscrew rookery of the National Audubon Society is one of the ornithological spectacles of the continent. There, in the labyrinth of islands, tens of thousands of nesting wood storks crown the mangroves like great blossoms.

Wood Stork

Lesser Yellow-Legs

[TRINGA FLAVIPES]

THE idyllic landscapes so frequent in his later pieces reflect Audubon's admiration of the Cruikshank prints. Here beside a woodland pool, a few miles distant from Charleston, South Carolina, he shows a "yellow-shank." In this spot he spent many pleasant hours with his friend John Bachman, resting after long fatiguing searches for birds in the surrounding woods.

In the lazy days of deep summer, from July on, the mellow whistles of yellow-legs drift over the tidal marshes that fringe the Atlantic coast. These slim waders are already southbound from the Hudson Bay country, and some will continue until they reach the wide marshy pampas of Argentina. Like so many other shorebirds, they have a tendency to migrate in a clockwise direction, returning in spring by a more inland route through the Mississippi Valley and the prairies.

Shorebirds are fascinating to watch when they swarm like sand fleas over the mud flats and the beaches, but they are a headache for the beginner to identify. The lesser yellow-legs, with its bright canary-yellow legs would be simple enough if there were not also a greater yellow-legs. The two differ in size: this one, the lesser, measures about ten inches long; the greater, fourteen. Experts, however, can tell them apart by their calls. Both are great tattlers, giving the alarm to all the shorebirds on the flat when someone approaches.

Lesser Yellow-Legs

Broad-Winged Hawk

[BUTEO PLATYPTERUS]

THE broad-wing, alone among the birds of prey, is a success story. Audubon, who knew this chunky crow-sized hawk, said it was by no means rare, but he leaves the impression that it was much less numerous in his day. It is evident that he never witnessed one of the massive migrations of broad-wings that go down the Appalachian ridges about the third week of September. At certain vantage points, such as Mount Tom in Massachusetts, the Kittatinny Ridge in New Jersey and Hawk Mountain in Pennsylvania as well as at focal points on the Great Lakes, it is possible in a single day to see thousands of broad-wings soaring in great wheels on the thermals.

This species seems to be prospering because everything about its life style and environment seems to work to its advantage. The second-growth woodlands that it frequents in the Northeast have vastly expanded as worked-out farms have been abandoned. Because of its food preferences (no small birds) it has escaped the perils of DDT and other chlorinated hydrocarbons in the food chain. And it escapes the autumnal gauntlet of gunfire by making a mass exodus from the United States before the hunting season starts. Furthermore, because of deforestation in the tropics (where the native hawks have declined) there is more second-growth for this species to hunt over during its winter sojourn. In Colombia, more than fifty percent of the birds of prey that one sees nowadays in winter are broad-wings.

Broad-Winged Hawk

Pileated Woodpecker

[DRYOCOPUS PILEATUS]

SECOND in size only to the mysterious ivory-billed woodpecker, the pileated woodpecker is still common in many parts of the United States. In some places, such as New Jersey, where it apparently disappeared some years ago, it has made a strong comeback.

This handsome woodpecker was my favorite bird during my youthful birding days, and it must also have been one of Audubon's favorites, if we are to judge from the imagination and effort that went into this spirited composition. He was of the opinion that it was even shyer than the ivory-bill and seemed to know the distance that shot would carry. This may partly explain why the pileated woodpecker survived and the ivory-bill did not, but a more likely reason lies in the food habits of the two species. The ivory-bill is a highly specialized feeder, the pileated less so. According to Dr. James Tanner, who did most of the research on the ivory-bill, it takes about six square miles of virgin timber to support a single pair of ivory-bills, whereas the same area will support about 36 pairs of pileateds.

Even when they keep out of sight pileateds betray their presence by their diggings, large oval or oblong holes, and also by their loud, irregular, flickerlike calls.

Pileated Woodpecker

Peregrine

[FALCO PEREGRINUS]

THE peregrine falcon, the finest bird that flies and perhaps the fastest, was the bird used most often in the medieval sport of falconry. Almost world-wide in distribution, it has become an endangered species on the North American continent.

Formerly known as the duck hawk, it has entirely disappeared as a breeding species south of Hudson Bay and east of the Rockies. This sudden collapse took place in the late 1950's and early 1960's when it became evident that the several hundred active eyries in eastern North America were no longer producing young.

It was discovered that the surviving birds were carrying in their bodies substantial amounts of DDT which in the females inhibited calcification, so necessary for egg production. They laid thin-shelled eggs from which few young hatched.

Today at Ithaca, New York, in the marvelous hawk barn adjacent to the Cornell Laboratory of Ornithology, Dr. Thomas Cade and his associates have been raising young peregrines from the egg, using captive stock from populations that still exist elsewhere in North America. The next step, which is now underway, is to take birds raised in this manner and establish them as breeders in suitable places in the East. The question remains: is the environment still so contaminated with chlorinated hydrocarbons that biological history will repeat itself?

Peregrine

Wild Turkey

[MELEAGRIS GALLOPAVO]

TODAY a single print of Audubon's wild turkey would bring at auction twenty times the original subscription price of the entire collection of 435 prints in the Elephant Folio.

In Audubon's day the wild turkey was still widespread east of the Rockies but already diminished or absent in some of the more northerly parts of its range which in colonial days extended to New England and southern Ontario. When he wrote the biography of this noble fowl Audubon noted that turkeys were becoming "less numerous in every portion of the United States, even in those parts where they were very abundant thirty years ago." He recalled that in earlier days in Kentucky he had seen birds of 10 to 12 pounds offered for three pence each and "a first rate turkey weighing from 25 to 30 pounds avoirdupois was considered well sold when it brought a quarter of a dollar." However, by 1836-7 they had risen in price to 75 cents in the markets of Washington.

By this time domestic turkeys were filling the void. These were descendants of wild birds of Mexican origin which had been brought to Europe by the conquistadors.

After domestication turkeys were returned to the continent of their origin.

After the wild stock had become much reduced in numbers, game management practices effected a comeback and today 1,500,000 wild turkeys are to be found in 47 states, including many areas in the West beyond the ancestral range of the bird. The National Wild Turkey Federation which is dedicated to the program of reintroduction and management now has a membership of 30,000.

Wild Turkey

Whip-Poor-Will

[CAPRIMULGUS VOCIFERS]

ON warm summer evenings the chant of the whip-poor-will rings through the leafy woodlands, a vigorous oft-repeated *whip-poor-weel* or *prrrip purr-rill*, with accents on the first and last syllables. Audubon said that "hundreds" could sometimes be heard calling simultaneously, surely an exaggeration, but there is no doubt that this well-camouflaged night bird is not as numerous today as it was within living memory. On my own 70-acre estate in Connecticut, an oak forest that has been spared by the axe, there were whip-poor-wills twenty years ago, but subsequent to a massive aerial spraying in our township about ten or twelve years ago their insistent voices have not been heard. Nor do we see the big saturniid moths on which they fed—the lunas, polyphemus and ios that formerly came to my studio windows at night.

I like Audubon's composition of the three whip-poor-wills because of its ecological information—the oak leaves where the birds find concealment during the day while sitting lengthwise on the branches, and also the moths on which they feed. He has depicted a cecropia and an io with the same fidelity that he has shown the birds.

Whip-poor-wills have a wide range from southern Canada through the eastern and central states to the Gulf of Mexico. They are also found in the Central American mountains from southern Arizona to Honduras.

Whip-Poor-Will

Common Eider

[SOMATERIA MOLLISSIMA]

AUDUBON has sometimes been accused by modern ornithologists of over-dramatizing his subjects. This animated composition of a trio of eiders risks this criticism, but it is almost certain that it was inspired by an incident that he had actually witnessed; perhaps during his Labrador cruise when he became very familiar with these striking sea ducks. Eiders are probably as abundant today as they were in Audubon's time, when they could be purchased in the Boston markets for 75 cents per pair. Although they are still hunted, they are no longer prized as much by wildfowlers and epicures. Great flocks numbering many thousands winter on the shoals of Monomoy on Cape Cod and many can also be seen offshore at Martha's Vineyard, but only a relative few reach Long Island. On the Maine coast and to the east in the Maritime Provinces they appear to be breeding in greater numbers than they did forty years ago.

Eider down, gathered from the nests of the sitting females, has long been an article of commerce. In Iceland, where eider farms are managed scientifically, the industry is an important part of the economy. With similar management, insuring the protection of the birds, the gathering of down could be profitable elsewhere because the species is found widely on both sides of the North Atlantic and North Pacific.

Common Eider

American Kestrel or Sparrow Hawk

[FALCO SPARVERIUS]

THIS beautiful little bird of prey is a falcon, not a true hawk as its obsolete name, sparrow hawk, would imply. Nor does it favor sparrows in its diet. Rather, it seems to prefer mice, grasshoppers and crickets which it spots from a high vantage point on some dead tree or telephone wire.

No other diurnal bird of prey except its larger relative, the peregrine falcon, ranges as widely in the New World. It is found from coast to coast and from northwestern Canada and central Alaska south through the two American continents to Tierra del Fuego. Adaptable, it is impartial to rural roadsides, open country, prairies, deserts, woodland edges, farmlands and even cities. It escapes persecution, to which the larger birds of prey are subject, by virtue of its size, hardly larger than that of a jay. When perched on a wire it looks somewhat like an oversized swallow. Even the slim pointed wings suggest those of a swallow rather than those of a typical hawk.

Unlike most other day-flying birds of prey it does not build a nest of sticks in a tree, nor does it lay its eggs on a cliff ledge. It seeks a cavity, usually excavated by a flicker, in some isolated tree or telegraph pole. In the desert a woodpecker hole in a saguaro cactus or a hole in a cliff will do. In the western foothills where holes are scarce it may appropriate an old magpie nest. Even a building in the center of a town may offer a safe nest site.

American Kestrel or Sparrow Hawk

Screech Owl

[OTUS ASIO]

AUDUBON has shown one gray screech owl and two reddish ones in this composition. He stated that the gray bird was an adult and the reddish ones were young. He was mistaken. Actually, these differences in color have nothing to do with age, sex or season. They are color phases. Red birds and gray birds may often be paired, or they may be the products of the same brood.

This wide-ranging little owl, found from Alaska and New Brunswick to Mexico, is perhaps the most familiar owl. Where barred and great horned owls dominate the night world, screech owls might be scarce, while in rural communities or towns, devoid of these large nocturnal predators which eat little owls, tree surgeons may be the screech owl's worst enemies.

In the eastern half of the continent, where screech owls come in two color phases, they give voice to a mournful whinny at night, a tremulous wail running down the scale. This call is easily imitated and the birds will often respond. In western North America, where they are either gray or dull brown, never red, screech owls do not have the descending whinny. Instead they sing a series of hollow whistles on one pitch, starting slowly then running into a tremolo with the rhythm of a small ball bouncing to a standstill.

Screech Owl

Whooping Crane

[GRUS AMERICANA]

TO Americans the whooping crane is the most publicized "endangered species." It is with some shock that we learn that Audubon himself killed seven with two shots, a remarkable feat inasmuch as these wary birds are almost impossible to approach if a man is carrying a gun.

In his biography of this species Audubon states that during its winter sojourn in the South it was "abundant in Georgia and Florida, and from thence to Texas." I myself saw the last of the wild Louisiana whoopers on New Year's day in 1948 when Bob Smith, the Mississippi flyway biologist of the U.S. Fish and Wildlife Service, took me out over the coastal marshes west of the Mississippi Delta in his two-seated patrol plane. For a brief moment our speedy little aircraft was not more than 200 feet away from the huge white bird as it towered above the flocks of snow geese.

There were less than three dozen whoopers in the world in 1948. By 1953 the number had dropped to about 23. Since then, due to the cooperative efforts of the National Audubon Society, the U.S. Fish and Wildlife Service and the Canadian government, the whooping crane population has climbed slowly but steadily to well over 100, including some in captive rearing programs. The main flock makes an annual journey from Wood Buffalo Park in northwestern Canada to the Aransas Wildlife Refuge on the central coast of Texas.

Whooping Crane

Canada Goose

[BRANTA CANADENSIS]

AUDUBON painted all of his birds life-size. This occasionally created problems of design when he endeavored to fit very large, long-necked birds within the confines of the page. In this Canada goose portrait he contrived to solve the dilemma by doubling back the neck and head. When drawing large long-legged waders such as the great blue heron and the flamingo he would drop the head toward the feet.

The Canada goose, like the robin, is a symbol of spring to those who are snowbound until March in the northern parts of the United States and in Canada. The returning flocks of geese are usually heard before their long wedges are seen in the sky as they knife northward. Large flocks travel long distances overland from the coastal bays, stopping only to rest and to feed. They may tarry awhile around the Great Lakes until the ponds and marshes further north open up.

Canada geese apparently bred widely in the northern states in Audubon's day, but by the beginning of this century few nested south of the Canadian border. In recent years resident populations have become re-established along the Atlantic seaboard at least as far south as Delaware and also at some inland localities. In general, geese are now doing very well; certainly better than some of the ducks, because they can graze in the stubble fields and are not as dependent on aquatic food. Enormous flocks congregate at some of the refuges such as Horicon Marsh in Wisconsin, sometimes creating problems on adjacent farms.

Canada Goose

Ruffed Grouse

[BONASA UMBELLUS]

THE ruffed grouse was obviously Audubon's favorite game bird, as it is today for many sportsmen. During his era there were no game laws that dictated the bag limit or the season when grouse could be taken. He himself shot them at all times of the year.

In former days the ruffed grouse was known as "pheasant" by country folk in the Appalachians and from thence westward, while in New England it was called "partridge." These names persist to this day amongst some sportsmen.

This large red-brown or gray-brown chickenlike bird of the brushy woodlands is usually not noticed until it explodes into the air with a startling whir. Two basic color types occur: reddish birds with rufous or reddish tails such as Audubon depicted, and gray or gray-brown birds with grayish tails. In the East, red birds are in the preponderance in the southern part of the bird's range which extends to the southern Appalachians, and gray birds predominate in the north. In the West, red birds are typical of the Pacific states, gray birds of the Rockies.

The "drumming" of the cock grouse is best heard in the early morning as it stands on a woodland log and beats its wings against its body. The muffled thumping starts slowly, accelerating into a whir: *Bup..bup...bup...bup...bup...bup...bup...uprrrr.* Audubon admits that he often lured drumming males to his gun by beating on an inflated bladder.

Ruffed Grouse

Wood Duck

[A I X   S P O N S A]

THIS, the most beautiful North American duck, actually was endangered in the eastern United States during the early years of the present century. The reason for its decline was that it remained throughout the eastern states during the summer; it did not migrate northward to less frequented lakes and marshes in the northern prairie states and Canada as did most other waterfowl. For this reason it was often known as the "summer duck." It was extremely vulnerable because spring shooting, not yet outlawed, went on at the very time that wood ducks were courting and setting up households. Things became so critical that the National Audubon Society (then known as the National Association of Audubon Societies) initiated a breeding program in Connecticut, raising birds under artificial conditions and setting out large numbers of nesting boxes for their convenience.

The wood duck does not nest on the ground or amongst the reeds as do most other ducks. It lays its eggs (up to 15 or more) in a tree cavity. Audubon occasionally found them occupying the abandoned holes of ivory-billed woodpeckers. Although a wood duck can squeeze into a hole that would seem too small to admit it, good nesting sites are often at a premium. To counteract this, game departments often build specially designed boxes, which are placed on poles several feet above the water where raccoons and other predators cannot reach them.

Baby wood ducks, a few hours after hatching, simply climb from the feather-lined nest to the entrance hole and jump out—even though it might be twenty feet or more above the hard forest floor. They survive and soon head for the nearest water with the rest of their nestmates.

Wood Duck

Greater Prairie Chicken

[TYMPANUCHUS CUPIDO]

WHEN Audubon was a young man in Kentucky he found pinnated grouse (prairie chickens) "so abundant that they were held in no higher estimation as food than the most common flesh, and no hunter of Kentucky deigned to shoot them. They were looked upon with more abhorrence than the crows." He reported that a friend who was fond of rifle-shooting "killed upwards of 40 in one morning, but picked none of them up, so satiated with grouse was he."

He added: "Such an account may appear strange to you, reader; but what will you think when I tell you, that, in that same country, where twenty-five years ago they could not have been sold at more than one cent a-piece, scarcely one is now to be found? The grouse have abandoned the state of Kentucky, and removed (like the Indians) every season further to the westward, to escape from the murderous white man." He reported that the eastern race of the prairie chicken (the now extinct heath hen) had become "so rare that in the markets of Philadelphia, New York and Boston, they sell at from five to ten dollars the pair." At that time they were still abundant on the midwestern prairies, but this too was to change, mainly because the bird could not adapt to modern agricultural practices. When the native prairie vegetation was eliminated they soon disappeared. Today the remaining populations, much restricted, are carefully managed. An organization in Wisconsin—*The Tympanuchus Cupido Society*—is dedicated to purchasing, preserving and managing remaining prairie chicken habitat.

Greater Prairie Chicken

Brown Thrasher

[TOXOSTOMA RUFUM]

AUDUBON'S dramatic portrayal of the thrashers and the black snake reminds me of his controversial painting of the mockingbirds defending their nest against a rattlesnake. The latter painting was much criticized by some of his contemporaries who averred that rattlesnakes did not climb trees. He was on safer ground when he adopted a similar concept for his painting of the "ferruginous mockingbird", as he called the thrasher. In this instance he showed a blacksnake, a reptile that does climb trees and which robs nests when it can. However, it is doubtful whether a second pair of thrashers would come to the aid of their distressed neighbors.

In Mexico there are many kinds of thrashers and their allies. Our southwestern states have eight, but in the eastern half of the continent we have only three—the brown thrasher, the mockingbird and the catbird. Audubon rated the thrasher as the most numerous songbird in the eastern states except for the robin. This certainly would not be true today. It is quite possible that thrashers have declined in the last century, but we lack measurable evidence.

Birds of the thrasher-mockingbird family are often called "mimic thrushes." Actually, the thrasher and the catbird do not mimic but have their own repertoire of short phrases. Whereas the mockingbird repeats each phrase a half dozen times or more before going on to the next one, the thrasher repeats but once. This pairing of phrases distinguishes its song from that of the catbird which does not repeat.

Brown Thrasher

Carolina Parakeet

[CONUROPSIS CAROLINENSIS]

THIS, the only parrot endemic to the United States, became extinct early in the present century; but in Audubon's day it was still so abundant that by his own admission he was able to procure a basketful of these birds with a few shots, in order to make a choice of good specimens for his drawing. He reported that farmers destroyed them in great numbers because of their crop depredations: "Whilst busily engaged in plucking off the fruits or tearing the grain from the stacks, the husbandman approaches them with perfect ease, and commits great slaughter among them. All the survivors rise, shriek, fly round about for a few minutes, and again alight on the very place of most imminent danger. The gun is kept at work; eight or ten, or even twenty, are killed at every discharge. The living birds, as if conscious of the death of their companions, sweep over their bodies, screaming as loud as ever, but still return to be shot at until few remain alive. I have seen hundreds destroyed in this manner in the course of a few hours."

Little wonder that Audubon was to write in his later years: "Our parakeets are rapidly diminishing in number, and in some districts, where twenty-five years ago they were plentiful, scarcely any are now to be seen. . . . I should think that along the Mississippi there is not now half the number that existed fifteen years ago."

Today it is still possible to see parrots in the United States, but they are not Carolina parakeets. They are escapees from the pet trade—monk parakeets and canary-winged parakeets from South America, budgerigars from Australia and half a dozen other species of exotic origin.

Carolina Parakeet

Osprey

[PANDION HALIAETUS]

TRADITIONALLY, the elegant osprey or "fish hawk," escaped the prejudice that condemned most other birds of prey. Ever since Audubon's day fishermen and farmers along the coast were of the opinion that an osprey's nest on the property was like a scarecrow, a warning to "chicken hawks" to keep away. Although there was nothing to this superstitious belief, it served to protect these large vulnerable birds from unnecessary persecution.

It was not until the post-World War II years that the osprey found itself in difficulty. The new wonder chemical DDT and related chemicals were being used widely and it soon became apparent that there was a connection between their use and the dramatic failure of many eagles, ospreys and peregrines to produce young. Chlorinated hydrocarbons are slow to break down and are passed along the food chain with a cumulative effect. Poisoned insects are eaten by small fish which are eaten by larger fish which in turn are easily caught by the osprey which transfers the accumulated poisons to its own tissues.

Although the afflicted ospreys were seldom killed outright by DDT, they laid porous thin-shelled eggs and reproduction dropped to almost nil. Where I live, near the mouth of the Connecticut River, this once abundant nester has almost disappeared. Now that chemical pollution is being controlled there is evidence that the surviving ospreys in nearby areas are again having some success in raising normal broods of two or three young.

Osprey

Black-Crowned Night Heron

[NYCTICORAX NYCTICORAX]

AT dusk on the marsh a flat *quok* or *quark* announces the arrival of the night heron from its hidden roost, perhaps several miles distant, where it has spent the day. Its silhouette against the evening sky is unmistakably that of a heron, but it is shorter-legged and stockier.

In recent years the large night heron colonies on Long Island and elsewhere in the northeast suffered a serious drop in numbers for reasons that are not fully understood. It has been suggested that the DDT syndrome of the 1950's and 1960's might have been responsible for the decline, but if so, why should the snowy egret, cattle egret and glossy ibis be prospering as never before? All three of these long-legged waders which share the night heron's marshes are now breeding in New England where they were unknown at the beginning of the century.

The black-crowned night heron is not peculiar to North America. It is a familiar inhabitant of marshes and shores from southern Canada to Tierra del Fuego and the Falklands where a dark race can be seen standing on the tidal rocks in the company of Magellanic penguins. It is also widespread in suitable terrain in Europe, Asia, Africa and some of the Pacific islands.

Black-Crowned Night Heron

Green Heron

[BUTORIDES STRIATUS]

THIS small dark heron is the most generally distributed member of its family in the United States and the one most likely to be seen around little wooded ponds and streams in the northern parts of the country. At close range it reveals a rich chestnut neck and greenish-yellow or orange legs. In strong light its somewhat iridescent upperparts may seem more blue than green, leading some inexperienced observers to believe they have discovered a little blue heron. Alarmed by close approach, it elevates a shaggy crest and flies off with a loud *skyow* or *skewk*. Airborne, it looks quite black and crowlike, but it flies with slower, more arched wing-beats than a crow.

Audubon has shown a green heron plucking a luna moth from the leafblade of a marsh plant, a rather unlikely incident because the ethereal green moth is usually to be found in a woodland environment. However, moths, like birds, have wings and therefore could be encountered occasionally in an atypical situation.

Whereas most other herons breed in colonies, the green heron tends to be a loner, usually nesting in the privacy of some thick grove or in an orchard, but there are places, particularly near the coast, where several pairs might nest together in loose association.

Green Heron

Ivory-Billed Woodpecker

[CAMPEPHILUS PRINCIPALIS]

THIS, our most spectacular woodpecker, may now be extinct. Recent sightings remain unconfirmed, yet in Audubon's day it was widespread and not uncommon throughout the swamp timber of the southeastern states. He reported that the crested head and white bill "forms an ornament for the war-dress of most of our Indians, or for the shot-pouch of our squatters and hunters. . . . on a steamboat's reaching what we call a *wooding place*, the strangers were very apt to pay a quarter of a dollar for two or three heads of this woodpecker." He adds: "I have seen entire belts of Indian chiefs closely ornamented with the tufts and bills of this species."

This relentless persecution took its toll, but environmental changes were the principal factor in the bird's disappearance. The ivory-bill needed large tracts of virgin forest where it worked mostly on trees that had been dead two or three years. It took about that long for decay to set in and the first insects to attack the wood—the fat whitish grubs of borers that tunnelled just beneath the tight bark. These grubs were the staple food of the ivory-bill. In another year or so, the subsurface borers disappeared. Decay ate deeper into the heartwood, and the ivory-bill was forced to look elsewhere for its special food which was becoming increasingly hard to find.

Ivory-Billed Woodpecker

Black Vulture

[C O R A G Y P S   A T R A T U S]

ALTHOUGH this composition may seem too macabre for the living room wall, it is, in my opinion, one of Audubon's very best. It is imaginative and brilliantly handled.

Although black vultures and turkey vultures may sometimes be seen together, they prefer to associate in assemblies of their own kind. The wide-ranging turkey vulture, which is found from southern Canada to Cape Horn, is the better sailplane of the two. Gliding effortlessly on long stiff wings, it rocks and tilts unsteadily to take advantage of subtle air currents.

The black vulture has a stockier look. It is readily identified by the short square tail that barely projects beyond the broad wings and by the whitish patches toward the wing-tips. Its flight is more labored than that of its redheaded relative—several rapid flaps and a short glide. The black vulture, which is the one most frequently seen around towns and cities in tropical America, seldom ventures north of Maryland and Ohio and avoids the higher hills and mountains into which the turkey vulture often ventures. At a carcass the black vulture is the more aggressive of the two. Both species have declined in recent years, although this is not well documented. They are struck by cars at roadside kills and some have succumbed to poisoned carrion.

Black Vulture

White-Crowned Pigeon

[COLUMBA LEUCOCEPHALA]

SOME of Audubon's finest compositions were painted during his stay in the Florida Keys where he noted pigeons and doves of a half dozen sorts. In those days they were shot and their nests pillaged until two species, the Zenaida dove and the Key West quail-dove, no longer came to the Keys from the West Indies. However, the white-crowned pigeon still makes the annual crossing from Cuba to nest in the mangroves and to feed on the sea grapes that grow in the Keys. The stronghold of this large pigeon is in the West Indies, but it can also be found locally on Cozumel and other Caribbean islands off the east coast of the Yucatan Peninsula in Mexico.

Undoubtedly the white-crowned pigeon owes its survival to its excessive shyness which Audubon noted when he tried to shoot some to use as models. Even so, he succeeded all too well, shooting 36 one day and 17 more the following morning. He reported that they arrived from across the Gulf Stream during the latter part of April. He watched several as they approached the shore, skimming low over the water, then rising to survey the country before pitching into the deepest recesses of the mangroves where he found it difficult to hunt them. Many years later, the great conservation society that bears his name gave warden protection to the diminished stock of this attractive pigeon.

White-Crowned Pigeon

Bald Eagle

[HALIAEETUS LEUCOCEPHALUS]

TO quote John James Audubon's account of the bald eagle in his *Ornithological Biography*: "The figure of this noble bird is well known throughout the civilized world, emblazoned as it is on our national standard, which waves in the breeze of every clime, bearing in distant lands the remembrance of a great people living in a state of peaceful freedom. May that peaceful freedom last forever!"

Since Audubon penned those brave words the Union has pushed westward to the Pacific. The bald eagle occurs in every state except one—Hawaii. Alaska, the 49th state, can boast far more bald eagles than all of the lower 48 states combined. There is also a very strong Canadian population.

Like the ospreys, bald eagles around the Great Lakes and along certain stretches of the Atlantic coast suffered from the effects of DDT and related pollutants, but with the ban on these biocides reproduction is now improving. However, eagles need space and only in Canada and Alaska do these big birds still find the elbowroom that they once knew.

Adult bald eagles with their white heads and tails can be instantly recognized. Not so the dark immatures which somewhat resemble golden eagles except for the whitish lining of the underwing. Audubon, in painting an aberrant immature bird, was under the mistaken impression that it was a new species which he named "The Bird of Washington."

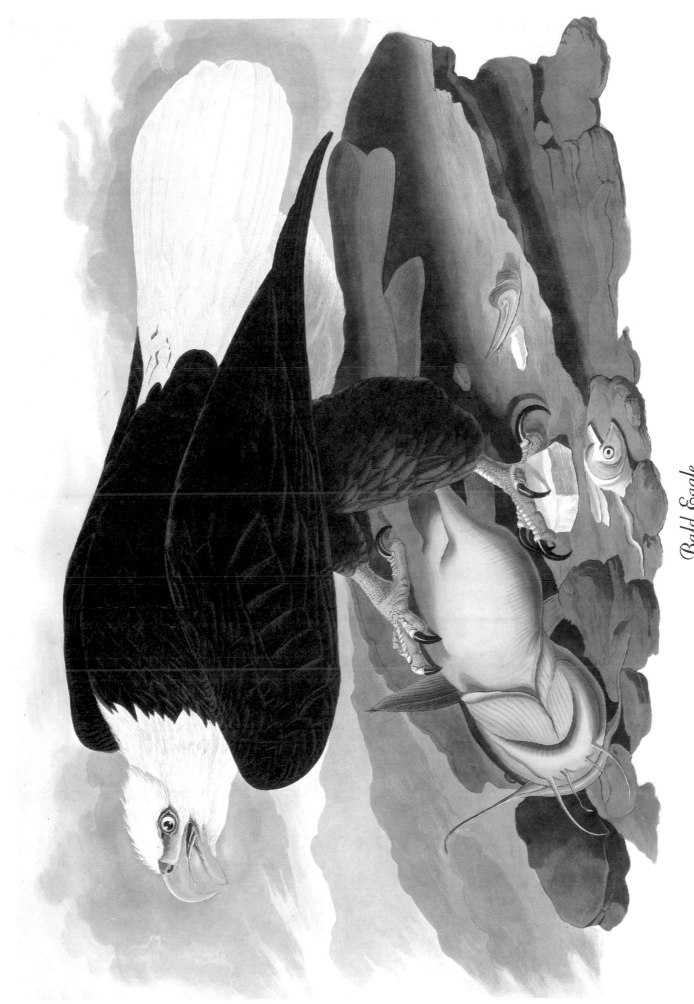

Bald Eagle

MOCKINGBIRD
(MIMUS POLYGLOTTOS)

CHUCK-WILL'S-WIDOW
(CAPRIMULGUS CAROLINENSIS)

NIGHTHAWK
(CHORDEILES MINOR)

JOHN JAMES AUDUBON could not have known that because of his superb artistry his name would become synonymous with the birds he loved. The great national organization that bears his name is dedicated not only to the protection of bird and other wildlife but also to their environment.

Audubon was, like many another successful genius, "the right man in the right place at the right time." He came to America as a young man with a fresh eye when it was still possible to document some of the unspoiled wilderness. He was also, during his lifetime, witness to the rapid changes that were taking place.

Not all of Audubon's bird prints are of equal merit or command equal prices. At a recent sale the print of the wild turkey was listed at twenty thousand dollars while certain other prints were offered at eight or nine hundred. This disparity may sometimes reflect the popularity of the subject matter rather than the comparative quality of the compositions. An eagle above the mantlepiece is more desirable than a vulture. A canvasback duck appeals more to the sportsman than a coot or "mudhen."

Some critics prefer those paintings in which Audubon eliminated the landscape, creating a bold design of the bird with a few vegetational accessories against a white background. In fact, the full environmental backgrounds, when he included them, were usually executed by his assistants.

The prints that I have selected are my favorites among the more than 500 portraits that were published, 435 of which appeared in his elephant folio edition of the *Birds of America*.

Illustrations continued on following pages . . .

FIELD SPARROW
(SPIZELLA PUSILLA)

SOOTY TERN
(STERNA FUSCATA)

BOAT-TAILED GRACKLE
(CASSIDIX MAJOR)

GREAT AUK
(PINGUINUS IMPENNIS)

BOBOLINK OR RICE BIRD
(DOLICHONYX ORYZIVORUS)

PIED-BILLED GREBE
(PODILYMBUS PODICEPS)

BARN OWL
(TYTO ALBA)

RED-SHOULDERED HAWK
(BUTEO LINEATUS)

CANADA JAY
(PERISOREUS CANADENIS)

BLACK-THROATED BLUE WARBLER
(DENDROICA CAERULESCENS)

UPLAND SANDPIPER
(BARTRAMIA LONGICAUDA)

PURPLE FINCH
(CARPODACUS PURPUREUS)

TRUMPETER SWAN
(OLOR BUCCINATOR)

MAGNOLIA WARBLER
(DENDROICA MAGNOLIA)

LEACH'S PETREL
(OCEANODROMA LEUCORHEA)

BAND-TAILED PIGEON
(COLUMBA FASCIATA)

PINE WARBLER
(DENDROICA PINUS)

BLUE-WINGED WARBLER
(VERMIVORA PINUS)

SEASIDE SPARROW
(AMMOSPIZA MAITIMA)

IVORY GULL
(PAGOPHILA EBURNEA)

PROTHONOTARY WARBLER
(PROTONOTARIA CITREA)

WHIMBREL
(NUMENIUS PHAEOPUS)

PARULA WARBLER
(PARULA AMERICANA)

LESSER SCAUP
(AYTHYA AFFINIS)

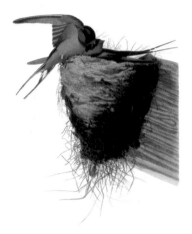

BARN SWALLOW
(HIRUNDO RUSTICA)

ALDER FLYCATCHER
(EMPIDONAX TRAILLII)

ZENAIDA DOVE
(ZENAIDA AURITA)